# Red List

# Blue

*poems by*

# Lizzy Fox

*Finishing Line Press*
Georgetown, Kentucky

# Red List

# Blue

Publisher: Leah Huete de Maines
Editor: Christen Kincaid
Cover Art: Alexis Avlamis
Author Photo: Steve Lausier
Cover Design: Elizabeth Maines McCleavy

Order online: www.finishinglinepress.com
also available on amazon.com

Author inquiries and mail orders:
Finishing Line Press
P. O. Box 1626
Georgetown, Kentucky 40324
U. S. A.

# Table of Contents

*For my parents.*

*I*

## *Hungry Ghost*

The woodstove curls its arms
around whatever creature sleeps

in the ashes; the ashes rise
and fall—breath around an ember,

a shrunken heart. I imagine
a cat or a baby raccoon

born of fire, a thin halo of smoke,
a snout warmed under a tail.

The house is cold.
I wish to be still

under blankets, wrapping my arms
around your chest, even when the dream

I slumber with is poor—filled
with pale faces and wide mouths flapping

like they're chewing all the time.
Ghosts with long

tickle-fingers. Parents forgetting
their children's names.

My alarm sounds like birdsong
whistling with the wind outside.

It's a cruel joke. I don't wish
for cheer. Just coffee. A little time

to myself, perhaps warming
my hands by the fire.

A woodstove is a stubborn god—
keeps its ashy babe comforted and small

while I sit and stoke
and stir and watch.

I wonder if you ever fear a chimney fire
when we leave the house alone

and burning, or awe
at the appetite of a woodstove

on a cold day—wood, wood,
more wood, and paper.

I could fill books
with my fears and hungers

and it wouldn't do me any good.
Alone, I balance small tinder, stuff

paper coils on the hearth's heart, blow
kisses until the flame licks

like it could warm me as well
as you do, until its low chimney-howl

joins the chorus outside. *We want more and more
and then more of it*, you say.

As if this were something I could stop.

# Beryl

*A heart is too stubborn to be a stone.* —Kyle G. Dargan

Though a stone may be carved in the shape

of a heart—polished, painted with an inspirational

quote and sold as a trinket, held in a worried palm.

A stone may be a heart, may be worried, may be

smoothed by the murmur of hands. "You worry me,"

says one. "I'm fine without him," says another.

A heart is too stubborn to take a river as it comes.

It is accustomed to controlling tides. A heart

is a moon circling another heart. A heart

does not abide a river. A river wears stones, chips them

until the edges are smooth and softened into dust,

until they can be carried. My heart—too stubborn

to be carried. A stone may join a river, careen

toward an ocean. An ocean may tumble cliffs into stone,

and then into sand, and then wash what-was-cliff

onto a beach where I lazily draw the letters

that mark your name, circling them over and over

like a whisper—something about loss. Oh God.

Let my heart be a stone.

## On Watching a Video of Sea Creatures Swimming through Trash

It's the stingrays that get me—in the aquarium's
touch-and-feel tank, how they look like improbable
birds or gentle dinosaurs. Their backs velvet-stained
rubber, toned muscle relaxed under a lover's grip.

Imagine: a kitten riding one like a horse
or snuggled under the flap as if it were a blanket.

My personal longings are one thing—how I always
wished to live by the sea but never did.

*We all buy things we don't need*, reads the caption,
folding us together in a cool sheet of shrink-wrap.

Spare earbuds protected in three layers of packaging
discarded on the car floor. Boxed rice. Individual
yogurt cups and seltzer cans. Extra plastic
grocery bags for tossing soiled cat litter.

Seagulls pick at old food on top of landfill heaps.
Their beaks pull up long strings of wire.

A tree in my backyard grows around a tire, giving
the illusion the earth will heal over our nonsense—
oceans so wide—just look at the tide come in.

## Small black candle

on a tea saucer, wax dripping over cream-colored
china, walls graying in its shallow light. The shadows

shift, and I shut my eyes, hum. A glacier melts
on the screen at the other end of the room. There are

five days of footage circling in the pixels. Ice cracks
and plunges into a cove. Seals bob up and down

to the mournful sound of ice and rain. I hum in just this
mournful way. The candle burns bright—melts away.

## On Anxiety (a definition)


I organize and reorganize piles of bills that I think, maybe,

I can't pay, but maybe I can if I stack them right, by priority

and deadline and likelihood of extension. I order and reorder

then reword each task on a task list, give the task list a name

like "Kitten Snuggles" to make it more appealing, then stay

in the office past 8pm to cross off each item. On a good day,

I feel accomplished: checking that the oven is off, then going

outside, then coming back inside to check that the oven is off.

I forget if I brushed my teeth or put on deodorant or locked

the door. I was thinking. Or scrolling Facebook. Or checking

my email on my phone. On a good day, I still notice

the smell of flowers, the movement of a cloud, the cardinal's shriek,

the chickadee's chatter. In summer I take walks, and I never sit down.

Winter is worse. The walking in my head. Some days, I write

"play with the cat" on a task list then watch endless cat videos.

Some days, my hands keep moving, and my mind is clear enough,

efficient enough. Days I feel solid, my head attached. Some days,

the air between my brain and the skull is pressurized, pushing out,

and the skull clamps down. Days my pulse is a sprint. A sprint. A sprint.

## Collapse

Tuna fish, fresh mahi mahi, balsamic reduction, scallops wrapped in bacon.
The resort had seven swimming pools next to the ocean and no reef-safe
sunblock. I swam over the reef wearing Banana Boat and cringing, flapping
my heavy flippers, breathing awkwardly through my mouth, wondering:
*where are the fish? Where are the fish?* I hand over my soggy excuses:
The family paid. Everyone was going. I'd been so sick.

All that trash in the headwaters. And the two of us filling the tub
in our hotel room, turning on the jets. There was a jacuzzi just outside.
There was a whole ocean.

I could talk about something cute—those miniature dolphins
dying. But it's not just the cute ones. See that man over there
with the sunburn? I could talk about fires, or the goats jumping from rock
to rock. How they eat everything in sight until soil slides into the sea.
How they were brought here on ships. I could talk about ships.
How akin they are to airplanes, and all that baloney in the in-flight
commercial—how flying brings cultures together. Voyeurs
and consumers. Swordfish on a plate. Linguini with lobster sauce.

## Blue

My jeans. The cover of this notebook. Pen ink.
My water bottle. The ocean. My eyes on sunny days

but not on cloudy ones. My tank top. You'd think
my favorite color would be blue, but I like red

and purple best. Shining jewel-tone reds,
and musty dusk-colored purples like the wash on a painting

by a man I love that's hanging in a gallery—or it was.
Last month. At the reception, the painter got drunk.

(I'm making assumptions. I wasn't there). He took
the bus home. He stood while the bus was moving.

When the driver stopped, the man I love flew forward
and cut his elbow on a sharp piece of metal.

He cut his elbow so deep the bone popped out.
He got stitches. He will sue. But I was telling you

about things that are blue: The bridesmaid dress
for my best friend's wedding. I will wear it

even though I'm the officiant. I agonized over the cut, wondered:
was it appropriate for the officiant to show so much cleavage?

She wanted me to write her a poem, but I don't write
about the kind of love you want mentioned at weddings.

I told her I'd find something someone else had done—
something suitable. I told her I'd read it really well

out loud. I do that—read things really well, out loud.
That's why she asked me to be the officiant

and her maid of honor—both positions that involve
giving speeches. The man I love slurred his speech

when he told me about his elbow. His speeches
are long, a trait we have in common. Once we went to dinner

and he spoke the entire time. He asked me why I never
tell him about my life. He's like my grandmother—he cannot

keep a secret. She was a painter too—my grandmother.
She dyed her hair red and used yellow washes to make

the canvas brighter.  She talked about the black hole
in her brain that ate memories. Later I learned

it was martinis. I'm beginning to notice a pattern.
The sky on a sunny day but not on a cloudy one. Sapphires

except not all of them. Did you know that sapphires
come in every color except red? Red sapphires are called rubies.

They're the same stone. Perhaps that bit was obvious.
I went on a blind date with a man named Amethyst.

When he asked what I was like, my friend told him to wear
bright colors and said he ought to bring me flowers.

So he taught himself to fold origami lilies and kept one
in his pocket until the end of lunch. It was the blue

of a robin's egg, which was the color of my grandfather's weeping
eyes when the cataracts set in but maybe a little darker.

Grandpa's eyes were ice-blue light shining—never cold,
not even when she was drunk and he was angry.

He remembered her sketches best. He wanted
his ashes buried with hers behind the church. But not all of them.

Some of his ashes would be spread, instead, from a sailboat
into the ocean, and inevitably of those, some would lift

over the water and be carried upwards—over our heads,
bone fragments sprinkling down again like rice.

## On Anxiety (a respite)

Occasional bursts of minor activity—peeling
the window's insulating plastic from the frame

pulling up the shade, killing a spider with a broom,
letting in the spring—lilacs and apple blossoms—

then, grating the cheese, baking the nachos. There's a slight
smell of burning that I know is the oven's floor, not yet

the cheese or chips, and nothing dangerous. You sniff
the air, glance at me with your head tilted, get up to check.

I enjoy your calm attention, the curve of your cheek as you lean
your face into the heat. Then you're back. Reading, pressing

your shoulder into my shoulder. Today, my heart is warm
and hums in my chest. Today it does not hammer.

## Collection

Three owls squat on the windowsill—one glass, one jade, one volcanic
stone—all gifts from my brother. They sit next to a curved
piece of pottery that Phil dug in the Balkans and smuggled
to Massachusetts. It's now a small dish displaying my grandmother's
worry doll, the hummingbird pin from dear Cynthia, and a trilobite
from my aunt's museum days curled in a perfect spiral.

On the desk, the woolen warrior doll from Chiapas
stands with her small wooden rifle, and the stuffed fox with its traveling bag
looks away from my father's pile of cardboard coasters, which he used
for a while, as small canvases—sitting at the bar with a rainbow of Sharpies
sweeping bright swaths of forest on fire, sunset over the lake,
and red-beaked birds. An occasional drop of beer is mixed

in with the landscapes. Hanging from the lampshade,
the old gold cross and the paper crane that came attached
to a Christmas gift from my mother twist at their strings.
*Here*, they seem to say, swinging in the pool of light, *Take this.*

## Bioluminescent

I sink through the water, down
to where sand firms underfoot. No wave
can move my body. Each wave moves me.
All around, the beach shines—waves
and sand up to the wrack line. I drift
like a whale filtering plankton through
baleen, their tiny bodies on my tongue,
in my blood, until my skin flickers blue
and green—I am a constellation, stars
over a new moon—my body a mirror
floating just below the waves.

## On Power

*"As a man's knowledge grows, and his power increases,*
*the road he takes grows ever narrower,*
*until at last he does only and wholly what he must."*
— *Ursula K. Le Guin*


Bicep, bone, bloodstream, esophagus,
coughing fits, apologies, laughter
in the vocal cords and a current of air—
a lamp sits on the table.

Plug it into the wall. Flip it on. Unplug it.
Reconnect. Be careful. You don't see
the current moving, but you know
it's there—a circuit.

You see a wire. A glimmer of light.
A backlit lampshade. A shadow.

A friend once gave a shadow-puppet show
in his living room, the paper cutouts
scissor-snip-precise and delicate, intricacies
intended to channel the light exactly
where he wanted it to shine:

eye socket, patterned shirt, in-between
strands of hair. Highlights in the dark.
Sometimes we are backlit.

Take a heart as example, or shock-pads
and monitors, or just the sound of a voice.

You don't see the current moving,
but you know it's there—a connection
to tend, to harness, to extend outward.

You see the body you were given, its intricacies
intended to channel the light exactly. You must.
Though you'll cast a shadow.

## Lovesick

The lip balm says, *Love Heals (Citrus Wood*
*Flavor)*, tastes like the slick inner bark
of an orange tree or a grapefruit stem
letting loose. Travelling, I watched a man knock
juice-swollen grapefruits from the boughs
straight onto the ground. "Too sour," he said.
"You don't want to eat those." Even as I protested
"I do! I do!" imagining how I'd cut them open,
dress the flesh in honey, squeeze the juice
straight onto my tongue.

## On Finding a Clam Shell at City Hall Park, Nowhere Near the Ocean

The broken edge shining in the grass, the pearly cup of it, the rainbow shine,
jagged, pale—like a thin stone. The wind cold on my back and bare feet as I bend

like when I hunted the wrack line for coral. There was a hunk the size of my head
and pale as the winter I'd run from. I searched the water for fish the colors

of these tulips: yellow and crimson and white, counted the swimming pools lined
along shore. Watched a Fritos bag blown off a balcony, spread the sunscreen,

saw the river run green and brown, the wind carry the bag into the water.
I tried to pull trash from the ocean. Tried to turn off every light, turn

baby sea turtles back out to sea, turn and turn and turn—the Earth
around the sun, and now it's spring. Even this changes in our hands.

See these trees? The shock of fuchsia blossoms. So well-tended, all in a row.

## On Anxiety (keeping busy)


Cat hair vacuumed, swept from corners
and from under the radiator. The top of the bureau
dusted with a wet cloth. Stovetop sponge-scrubbed.
Dishes dried and stacked and all the clutter
tucked. Books straight. Paid bills and pay stubs
and bills-to-be-paid-online and electronically
deposited checks—shredded. One by one. Sheets
stretched on the bed. Stuffed owl sat upright. A candle
lit, blown out. The dishcloth wrung. The chairs
slid under the lip of the kitchen table. All the pens clicked
shut and stowed in the pen cup. The calendar flipped
(finally) to the right month. Pillows fluffed. I'm ready.
I'm waiting. I ate all the french fries without you. I won't
do it again.

## *Almost*

We are tender. Only fools watch from a porch
while meteorites the size of thumbnails fall
quiet, each one glowing like a soft torch.

They singe the lawn before they quit, scorch
the dirt, then—no more than fallen marbles.
We are tender fools enclosed in a porch.

Your nose presses into my cheek, forehead forced
on my temple, fingers hold the hollow
of my throat. Each point glows quiet—a torch.

The lights are leaving. I want to wind a course
through their shower, catch them like fallen
flakes on my tender tongue. Fools on a porch.

While neighbors dance under a lit sky, you pour
a whisper, hold me easy as a lie about beauty, all
your fingers glow quiet. Everything is torched.

I don't love you—certain as stone, that source
of knowing in my belly, a weight appalled.
We are too tender—only fools watch from a porch
while the sky glows quiet like a soft, guiding torch.

## Trying to Write an Essay

I stare at my laptop and say, to no one, "It's silly."
It's silly, crying like this. I'm trying to write an essay.
I have the same fantasy over and over: the animals come back.

Is that all? I say, "I don't know."
Another month will pass. I'll forget.

A balloon caught in a tree outside the window
bobs up and down. It will shrivel behind the leaves.

I search each end
of the word, turning it over in my brain: *return*
*return*
*return*. A strange noise from across the meadow:

"Is someone shooting fireworks?"          No.

## On Depression (a sticking point)

On the back of the tongue where a pill
will stick if it's not washed down,
where if it sits long it starts to burn,
where, melting, it tastes like bitter chalk.

That kiss at our friends' wedding.
Each of us alone. Who knows

what you wanted. I try not to say your name:
a handful of pebbles. Iron and ginseng.
Fish oil. Uncoated Tylenol. I chew
dark greens topped with walnuts I crush myself
under a heavy knife.

## Leaving Home

I thought a long time about this—how to dice
the vegetables, the balance of sauce and cheese

and protein, the number of meals left, the weight
of each Tupperware. Have you ever felt, just, wretched

where you are? My bed is for sleeping and sleeping in.
I move slow on my way to my job—a beaver lumbering

on land, seeking new waters to dam. I love
a project. The way it eats the hours, makes me feel

almost hare-like. My mother taught me to move carefully—
to pack each dish in paper.

## Cowboy Camping

Moon beams split through the leaves. Branches shift
in a high wind. There's no relief on the ground. A critter
nearby stirs, and that's all. Nothing but a thin veil of plastic
beneath me. I've no roof. A group of Ivy Leaguers lent
their tarp after they took the whole lean-to. The critter
is bigger than a chipmunk but smaller than a bear.

Porcupine, if I had to guess. There's no one to guess to.
The moon spots like a disco ball spinning. I pull
the sleeping bag over my face. The last time I did this
I was nearer to the mountaintop. It was earlier
in the summer. I was with an old boyfriend.

We woke at dawn to heavy hoof-steps. An adolescent moose
loomed over our bodies. We stared at the great underbelly,
the flies swarming its face, the roaming look
of its large brown eyes trying to make heads or tails
of the nearby shelter we'd foolishly abandoned. The moose
was panting. A foot-long stream of drool hung dangerously
over my boyfriend's neck. When I stopped swearing, I started to pray.

I hope the porcupine isn't curious. I hope the wind doesn't carry rain.
I hope if it does, it blows north into the open side of that lean-to.

The moose walked calmly past our bodies once it had caught its breath.
It slipped beyond the trees. I placed a hand on my boyfriend's chest,
but he ran away—said he needed to release adrenaline. I took
out my journal and wrote it all down. My denial.

That's not rain I hear tapping on the tops of the leaves.
I am not afraid of porcupines.
The trees will keep me dry.
I am not angry with the students. I am not alone.

## Empty / Full

The branches, the ground, the frost in your hair
all become lattices, ladders of spiral-stretched frost
crystals reaching like dancers in tiny white gowns,
their arms up. Even my breath climbs. See?

It spins up to your mouth when I look at you—
framed, like everything, in the faux-fur
of my oversized hood. Your body steams. Sweat breaks

through your jacket, brightens the peaks of your cheeks.
And your grin at the top of this climb—how it thaws
my toes and fingers, my nose tucking in close to your nose.
Before, winter was only dark. Full with shivers.

Have you seen how the light bends off the ice these days?
The way snow becomes the sun? How empty the trees,
always reaching, never in want?

*II*

## Certitude of Motion

This morning, a pileated woodpecker
with its enormous red crest flew low
over the roof of my car while I moved

down the highway in slow commuter traffic.
I flinched as though it might crash into my hair.
Thank God it stayed in the air!

Once, another woodpecker zipped into the trees
inches ahead of a passing truck. The driver
bore down on his brakes to barely miss it, but later,

biking back by the same spot
I spied a pool of blood and red feathers
lying in the middle of the road.

At my desk, arrived and unharmed,
I listen now to a hammer swing and knock
against a nail in the nearby lumberyard.

I swear I can hear it—the knocking of its body
against my windshield, the body falling from the sky.

## Cage Crinoline

*It's estimated that in 1860 three thousand women burned to death largely due to the flammability of hoop skirts.*

Ballerinas were particularly vulnerable, the tarlatan
and gauze. But all girls could light like chimney fires—

the bells of their hollow hoop skirts funneling air
up the legs. In the days of fireplaces and gas

stage lamps, don't dance so close. Three thousand
women burned that year catching a hem, tipping a candle.

The fabrics were spiderwebs and angels' gowns.
The women—dried-out Christmas trees, needles

dropping. It was before household electricity,
but mass-produced fabric meant every girl

could leap like Emma Livry. See them
at their mirrors, pretending, making

pouty expressions with eyelashes spread—
the slightest mis-gesture led to death.

Ballerina skirts were longer then, and light—
made to look like seraphs. Everything was white

or lavender or buttercup and paid for by old male patrons
championing his girl to the top of a playbill. Once,

a whole row lit in formation. The one on the end—too close
to the lamp. The others—too close to the girl beside her.

A new dance began.

The same dance when one sister rushed to the fireplace
to put the other out. The trouble with hoop skirts

was that women could move their legs.
They burned down brownstones,

apartment buildings, theaters, lost
icons, lead dancers, soft faces, those long-carved limbs.

She was waiting for a casting call, stressed, sneaking
a cigarette—had just gotten the tobacco lit when he approached.

      She'd insisted on warming the house with her husband
      gone to work and the children away.

           She needed the candle to find her bedchambers,
           brought it right into the room. It cast light
           on her smile, her bodice, her undone button.

She was facing the wall, about to breathe in—turned
and tucked the flame quickly behind her back
so he wouldn't see. You could almost hear the suck of air
pulling inside and up.

           She brought the candle to her own bedside

      after all

      insisted on doing things alone

had the audacity to dance

           was trying to help her sister.

## On Damage

Trying to parallel park, I almost pull into an oncoming pickup,
then, angered by failure—roaring and roaming the block
for a new space—I bite my finger so hard I break skin. I clip
a wart off my knuckle. It bleeds and bleeds. My cat—kneading
the blankets—hooks a claw into my buried wrist, jumps up
to the window so my skin tears. She didn't mean to. My neighbor
slams a door, a glass down, a chair across a room, screams at his wife.
Outside, their kids play statue-tag, careful to avoid the glitter of bottle glass
broken across the side yard. I had a full yard when I was a kid.
And bottle glass, too. So much glitter, my skin still shines.

## Slant Light

*"Tonight is the night of the full untrustworthy moon."*
—Mary Ruefle

My mother outside our yellow house, her boots
punching through snow as she walks
slowly further.

                         Or is it my father?
Pointing to the lunar eclipse, holding my shoulders and smiling
even as he sighs in that loud way of his—warming his voice
for a tired solo, a ragged lament.

She left him then. Or asked him to leave. Or was it I
who wandered off? *Tonight is the night*, she said
and either way we scattered.

I imagine my eyes as yellow as the light slanted
cold through the window. Tomorrow, the moon will wane.

I've forgotten all other names and pray to the harvest—
for bounty to come in on snow. I'm told abundance
means welcoming all of it—memory, loss, regret.

The snow is bright against my window—constancy, movement,
fracture. The moon will become a sliver and a shadow,
then nothing at all, hiding among the stars.

# My last lover asked me if I was an insomniac

but I just couldn't sleep
there under skylights,
floor-to-ceiling windows
reaching up to the third
loft where he'd perched
the bed, tree branches
and light pollution gray
around us like the sun
was still out behind clouds.
I rose naked and stood
by the bannister, looking
over his strange city
feeling like a mayor's wife
or a millionaire. I thought
I could get used to it—
the opulence, his iridescent
gaze. When he looked
I thought *I am held*
*in beauty*, held in place
by soft, wide wings trying
to assure me his charm
was more than the right notes.
It was silent
when he slept. He fell in
fast—rolled away from me
in slumber, kept his hands
to himself, a space of air
between our bodies. I sang
like a bird in morning when
finally, he rolled back stiff
and ready, wanting to know
what thoughts had kept me up.

## Undefined

The first clearing we've seen in weeks—small—
a blue-sky morning over half the yard. Snow

still floats in shifts—miniature paper cranes sent
on an angled air current, then held.

Sent down. Then held.

Crows perch on the tangled branches
of a fallen tree. A blue jay on the edge of the woods

tricks my eye a moment, seems to be
something larger. Remember lying on your bed

under the skylight, among tree boughs, wondering
at the underside of giant jay—could it be a hawk?

But no, wrong color. I felt safe exclaiming with you,
falsely, over backyard wildlife.

It seemed such a normal moment, one for lovers.

## Impossibilities

We sit by the fountain, water loud and artificial like rainwater
pouring out of a gutter after a storm. Never the storm itself.

A young father approaches with his little girl. She wears indigo eyeglasses.
"Why doesn't the water spill out of the pool, daddy?"

He explains about pumps and drainage, a constructed water cycle, a kid's
science project made of cement and wrought iron. Her laughter

hits the fountain like a handful of pennies thrown against metal.
"Magic!" She screams. Weren't we just talking about this?

Pointing to the grass and to the bench and saying, "This is god,
and this is god, and this is impossible?"

And weren't we just singing that one line of a song on repeat:
"Every little thing she does is magic"

while gesturing to the lawn and to the sky and holding handfuls of earth
up in our fists? A dull and quiet bird

flies into a low branch above our heads, her profile impossibly
long and thin. "Look at that bird!" I say, struck and wishing

I knew more Latin, more names to call the world by. "Where?
I don't see it." The bird is darkened by the effects of bright sun

and tree shadow. "Magic! Magic!" The girl screams, splashing her hand
in the water, climbing in and stomping around the pool which reaches up

to her impossibly small thighs. Her father is afraid, perhaps, of enthusiasm.
Of erratic and fervent joy. Of unclassified objects. Of getting wet.

"It's not magic," he snaps, pulling her from the pool, away.

A ladybug crawls toward your hand, and I think
*luck is another word for magic.* You place
an index finger on my arm: "Absolutely impossible."

## How to Make Art

Even when I'm sick, when I feel
the thorn of a sore throat
prick my right tonsil, and I hiss
through a stuffed nose
while I dream of spilling my coffee
because I'm stumbling
through the house without opening
my eyes because I can't open
my eyes because I'm still dreaming
and I'm late for work, I hear
the robin's circular whistle
at the window. Winter is always long.
But the robin is back. Even
when the weather won't stand still,
when it throws my body
into viral confusion with snowstorms,
hailstorms, and sixty-degree winds
all in one week, the robin is building her nest.
The robin has work to do. She is singing.

## The Gamble

Though it could close her airways to bite
into the greenery, my new kitten beats playfully
at the peace lily I'd hoped she would avoid.

Her white paws are rapid fire. The elephant
ears bend and drum as if shaking in rain.
Her eyes twitch. Her tail tip cuts smooth
through the air—left, then right. She opens
her jaws, and a passing puff of dust distracts her.

Now, she's a wild thing crouched beneath a leaf.
I follow her gaze—look where she looks—the gray
beyond the window. A day so hazy, anything
could be there. A white Bengal tiger
stalking an elephant in the neighbor's driveway,

the elephant flapping her ear like a flag
in mist. In the swimming pool, a shark fin
splits the water. Everything goes gray gray gray.

Coming up from the bottom of the deep end, a mermaid
hits her highest note, wagering her voice away.

## Glitter

She holds herself solid, supple. Swings her arms through the air. We gasp and gape at the right moments, wonder at the glint of light off her sequined costume, at the tight stretch of her smile. I drag my eyes down the curve of her waist all the way to her partner's biceps and think, *Of course. All it takes is the right man to make her fly.* It's a small assumption, almost unconscious. How still she gets—her thighs flexed between his fingers, her wrapped abdominals lifting her weight into the air until she's almost nothing between his hands. I remember flying. Tossed into the air by my father— how I wanted to sparkle so bright I'd become a little winged Cinderella, flying up toward light until I disappeared. How hard—I learned—what work it was to squeeze delight all the way into the air. It's our job to make the lifting easy. He lets her down to the stage where she sinks into a split, glances past our astonished faces, gathers her body into a low spin.

## *On Anxiety (cortisol)*

All the music turned down, the buzzing of a beehive
between my ears. Except that's not right. The bees are dying.
*Aren't they still?* The way they swarm and disappear. *Maybe
it was the coffee?* A tight helium balloon in place of my lungs.
A nest of baby snakes in my belly. A cirrus cloud, icy and stiff
and far away. Impending lightning. A mumbled curse
behind the wheel. *I should run more.* The frown line
between my eyebrows. *Concentrate, concentrate
concentrate.* A little girl's magic spell. A chant. A wish
to be lighter. *I could try meditating.* Try reading fiction.
Try watching movies. Try drinking water. Try a therapist
or a friend. Try a walk around the block. Try cleaning. Try
to slow the heart. Place a hand there and feel it. Blood flow,
adrenals out-of-control. *Somehow I can fix this.*

## Armadillo Child

In the field, I am always
sad. Always looking inside
my mind and up to a blue
tainted sky. Cumulus
clouds, scattered and solitary,
billow up like armadillos, each
lumbering its own slow
and dusty path, not threatening
to gather. In the field, on the ground,
lying amidst hard, scratchy grasses
I am alone but for long black
caterpillars that measure me
in my feinted sleep. There,
I am a daydream—not of armadillos, nor
any other confined and hard-shelled
thing—but of a far-flung future,
a gathering of bodies, a mapping of ties.
In this dreamt-up bliss, I am not
discontented, not easy to anger,
not alone here, nor empty.

## Monarch Meadow

The round hay bales ran over with baby garter snakes—
olive and yellow ribbons that slid over our palms, the lot of us

competing to see who could be the most indifferent, who
could hold the snakes without flinching. Of course I didn't win.

Sleek-striped caterpillars crawled in masses over grass
and milkweed. When I was alone, I closed my eyes to dream of growing.

Time moved the way a rainbow fades while caterpillars
silently measured my limbs and the strands of my hair,

mapped my neck and ankles. They gave way to monarchs. So many
we gave the meadow its name and kept it long after the monarchs

left. Back then, the air was so orange and shifting, it may have been a flame.
Summer was slipping. A residue hung in the late afternoon, then fell.

I left before night came on but imagine the field filled with fireflies in summer
and in winter, only ghosts—the same ghosts my brother said

came into the house at night to shatter bottles and leave holes in the walls.
We both left on bedside lamps so as not to endure the dark, and I'd lie awake

for hours, listening. In daylight, I could hold the future. I was sure.
I did not know the new farm would pick apart the bales and till the milkweed
            under.

That monarchs would starve mid-migration.
That they were half-ghosts already, fluttering before my eyes.

# Gray

It is the black of the morning. A crescent moon, bright
like it were full, assaults my window. My eyes

squint open. Black sky. Yellow stars. White snow.
*Why am I awake?*
It should be night, but my alarm sounds 6am.

\*


It is gray-light when I force myself from the covers, groggy,
foggy-headed, and angry I've missed pre-dawn,
the calm before anyone stirs, the silent hour,

before even birds. There were nightmares in the black.
I thought if I finished them, they wouldn't seem so bad.

\*


The gray dissolves. A drop of orange dye disperses
yellow, then white, then winter-blue.

The snow crossed with deer tracks.
The cloud of my thoughts thick and weighted.

I know what you're thinking: *all this over sleeping in?*
It's a common mistake—the slipping of time
like dropping a water glass from a fevered hand.

All those shards—fractured light
skitter-scatter—impossible to put back.

## On Depression (a reckoning)

There's this lump aching
under my vocal cords—like a stone,
but not a stone—a rubber ball
rolling in fractional rotations
from one side of the throat
to another—but, no, softer
and gummy—a dried-up
wad of rubber cement, wedged
higher now, near the tonsils. I swallow
and swallow, but it will not go down.

It's been there for a week.

Tea, coffee, ice cream, soda water, water water, honey, salt,
a slice of lemon wedged between my lips, breathing
steam in hot showers through deep belly-breaths my father
taught me during tantrums, standing in the rain mouth open to the sky,
sweet clover growing on the roadside with its familiar tang, tree-climbing
until I'm sure the air is lighter, singing my scales up there among
the leaves, screaming prayers, beating my fists against a branch, peppermint
candies, and more—begging the tears to come.

The stiffness in my lower back. The neighbors shouting again: it's after midnight.
The whirring of a box fan. The rumble.

No matter what I do, I hear myself say: *Not that.*

## *Updating the Red List*


*Extinct, Extinct in the Wild, Regionally Extinct, Critically*
*Endangered, Endangered, Vulnerable, Near Threatened—*
The Red List a menagerie of unpronounceable Latin,
pixelated faces, tree limbs, ferns. I click and drag each picture
to its place, count the lost and the losing, guess

genus and region by common name before I read the notes.
It's easier with my silent game—pretending I can win.
I like to open the window while I work, listen to the birds.
I tell myself it's not just a funeral song, no elegy.
Someone will listen.

So I read and type and try not to memorize the names,
try not to say them with my full voice. Ever a whisper.
The birdsong grows quieter each morning.
At the bottom of each page a button says, "Show More."

# Broken Thorn Sweet Blackberry: A Boy's Memory

*In response to Brigit Pegeen Kelly's "Song"*

Listen: I can't get your name
out of my head—a gentle stroking,
the rhythm of a girl's fingers in my hair.
The hair was matted with blood.

That morning, all I wanted: one berry
ripe in the middle of the bush
uneaten by birds—a thorn broke.
A prick of blood under my nail.

Who sings the song?

I hear it at night. A broken thorn
stuck in a tangle of girl's hair, in a mat
of animal fur, lying in the dirt
under a songbird's small talon.

Blackberries aren't usually sweet.
Only when they're overripe, when the sun
softens them to premature jam—
then they are worth eating.

Listen: I don't know who keeps the music
going. Same tune every night—a bird
with a thorn in its foot, something sweet.
Does that even happen?

I can't tell you anything you don't
already know. An animal was in the yard.
It wouldn't stop bleating.
I wanted to hold the quiet sky in my arms,

but it was far, and the clamor of feet,
of knife-on-fur, of hard breath
made me forget the sky for a while.
The knife was sticky, slick,

dripping thick as if with jam.
I wanted one of the other jobs:
to hold the animal's feet so it wouldn't kick
or its mouth so it wouldn't bleat

but they whispered my name and clapped
my back. When I got home, my shirt
was dotted in rusty fingerprints and streaks.
I buried it under my mother's rosebush.

Listen: when the night began, I was alone.
And when I went to bed, alone again.
And in school all the next day and the day
after that, I spoke less to the others

but never stopped. When the night began,
I was whistling. The first star came out and winked
to the tune of my song. There was a bird at dusk.
We had a call-and-response. I don't know why

we did it. I kicked a stone at the goat-post, said
*I wish it would stop.* I didn't say
*Get me a knife.* But they did
that night, and every night after on repeat.

One boy's smirk. My small nod. Somewhere
my bird's whistle too soft to hear.
And here's the worst part: I've done it
over and again. Just yesterday I brought a hen out.

She'd stopped laying, and I taught my boy.
He drew the knife. I held her wings.
We didn't even need the meat.
Just wanted more space in the coop.

Sometimes the song sounds like the goat
and sometimes it sounds like the girl
and sometimes, now, it sounds like a hen
squawking or field of cicadas gone

quiet under a crop-duster's spray. Tonight, it sounds
like my son—the way he hummed while he worked
and screamed when the blood hit his pant-leg.
I almost taught him to enjoy it.

## Tail-End of Mourning

I wake up late and lonely, cloud-light
showing through the shades in stiff
horizontal lines. Hollow air.

My neck aches from the pillow.
On cold mornings it is easy to slip
into loneliness, to forget.

There is a well with clear water
at the base of my spine waiting
for me to remember. I shut my eyes.

Waves lap my tailbone: *Remember,*
each whispers. One, then another.
I reach for a pen, barely able

to flex my fingers, tempted to lie
down and layer blankets over my shivering
frame. I press ink onto the page. A wave

down my forearm. *Name them,* it says.
There is a glass of water on my nightstand.
I take a drink and write your name.

## Writing

Sometimes I skip pages in my journal
like skipping rocks, except I can go back
and fill them in.

And gravity will not sink them.
They're buoyant—my thoughts—
and the spaces in between them.

A friend's mother owns a cottage
on a pond which is being slowly overgrown
with lily pads. One day, it will be a marsh
and the dock will be drowned in mud.
The frog-song will be exquisite.

I go there, sometimes, to this
future marsh—and it doesn't matter
that I live in a city,
or that my nightly serenade is the neighbors'
drunken squabble, or that the frat boys
spill out across the street shooting
each other with pop guns—there is a marsh
I go to, filled with bullfrogs. The water
is closed in with reeds, and sometimes fog,
and always you are there
with your small stone, and the thin path
you create, magically, through the water.

## Making Light

Warm in the air, wet
in the dirt: first rain.

From my bones lifts
the hurt of winter. Rain

hums in the gutters, keeps time
on the roof. Inside,
I hum a simple tune:
a garden, long days, dark dirt.
I hum and the room expands—
no walls, no wind.

I shape a lamp from hammered
copper and place it in the space.
I leave it with the switch clicked on
and wait—sunlight pours
onto the floor. All through the room
it spreads—the light.

## A minute to seven


and the light comes up misty,
rained upon, still sounding of crickets.

All night I woke on and off to their trill
and the fear that I'd rise too late to write—

the only practice I know to hold
with my small and sufficient god.

But I came to on time, and as I finish
this pre-dawn séance, the garden

emerges out the window. The rain falls
barely. My cat listens at the door

for the scratch of my slippers,
my rousing to feed her.

I've sat here for more than an hour
and am quietly in love with the morning.

Whatever terror is in the world today,
may we meet it with a gentle rise.

## Valentine's Day

I pluck the last truffle from a heart-shaped box. Caramel sticks to my teeth—
sends a sugary shock. I've never married. In the shower, I twist my back
to see skin crease at the love handle. I let water run hot down the side
of my neck and see the puckers on my buttocks like pockmarked marble.
I dance when I walk. I hold each pose as if I were a model. I'm
the anticipation of small births—the burst of tulip petals, geese come north.
Soon: arrival. I prepare for divorce from winter, walk aimlessly,
find myself beneath the hummingbird mural. Its ruby throat beckons me
to climb up and drink. I'm afraid of heights. Living on the ground,
I see small things: the child who licks cherry goo from her fingers,
the discarded candy wrapper stuck in a wad of snow sure to melt,
puddles growing like so many small prayers.

## Notes on the Poems

*Cage Crinoline:* I owe the information and storylines in this poem to the article, "A History of Women Who Burned to Death in Flammable Dresses" by Rae Nudson, published in *Racked 2017.*

*Hungry Ghost:* The italicized lines are from Marie Howe's "What the Living Do."

*Impossibilities:* The quoted song lyrics are from "Every Little Thing She Does is Magic" by the Police.

# Acknowledgments

I wish to thank the anthologies, journals and exhibitions where these poems have previously appeared, sometimes in earlier versions, including:

*Aurochs:* "Broken Thorn Sweet Blackberry: A Boy's Memory," "On Finding a Clam Shell at City Hall Park, Nowhere Near the Ocean," and "Updating the Red List"
*Aurora Poetry Anthology by Allegory Ridge:* "Almost"
*deLuge Literary and Arts Journal:* "Monarch Meadow"
*The Greensboro Review:* "Hungry Ghost"
*Hunger Mountain:* "Cage Crinoline" (under the title "Fashion, 1860") and "On Power"
*Hunger Mountain Online:* "Cage Crinoline," "On Power," and "How to Make Art"
*Lily Poetry Review:* "Lovesick"
*PoemCity Montpelier:* "Bioluminescent"
*PoemTown St. Johnsbury:* "Armadillo Child"
*The Pomeroy Poets Anthology:* "Small black candle" and "Valentine's Day"
*Puerto Del Sol:* "My last lover asked me if I was an insomniac"
*River River:* "Beryl"
*Santa Ana River Review:* "Making Light"
*Small Orange:* "On Watching a Video of Sea Creatures Swimming through Trash"
*The Spirit It Travels: An Anthology of Transcendent Poetry* (Cosmographia Books, 2019): "A minute to seven" and "Writing"
*The Worcester Review:* "Slant Light" and "Undefined"

Thank you, also, to the many friends, colleagues, and mentors who helped shape this manuscript. I can't possibly name all of you, but I will try. I am grateful to my VCFA advisors, Leslie Ullman, Tomás Q. Morín, Nance Van Winckel, Cynthia Huntington, and Jamaal May at the Postgraduate Writers' Conference; to the abundance of readers who looked at poems in various stages, including: Rick Agran, Julianna Baggott, Lisa Buckton, Duncan D. Campbell, Karen Cygnarowicz, Lennie Decerce, Cameron Finch, Samantha Kolber, Sarah Leamy, Matthew Olzmann, Meg Reynolds, Aja Zoecklin, and everyone from the Pomeroy Poets; and to those who have offered their encouragement and support, including: Rita Banerjee, Emma Bast, Ayse Bayar, Jeremy Blanchard, Ann Dávila Cardinal, Chanel Dubofsky, Rajnii Eddins, Miciah Bay Gault,

Tavia Gilbert, Geena Glaser, Robin Largesse, Ellen Lesser, Erin Stalcup, Zo Tobi, Josh Van Vliet, the entire VCFA community, everyone at the Academy for Coaching Excellence, the Clarkies (you know who you are), El Puente, and so many more. If I missed you by name, please accept my apologies and know that I am sending you all my gratitude nonetheless. Special thanks to Finishing Line Press and to my editor, Christen Kincaid.

Always, thank you to my dearest mentor, the late Cynthia Emerlye. Rest in peace.

To my parents and to Granny: this book would not be without you. Thank you for cheering me on, for being generous, and most of all, for raising me to love and keep loving.

Finally, to Steve, who supports me in more ways than I imagined possible. I am so lucky to have found you.

## *About the Author*

**Lizzy Fox**'s poetry has appeared in *The Greensboro Review, Hunger Mountain, Puerto Del Sol,* and elsewhere. In 2013, she received the Laura J. Spooner Prize for Best Love Poem and the Corinne Eastman Davis Memorial Award for Best Poem from the Poetry Society of Vermont. Lizzy holds an MFA in Writing from Vermont College of Fine Arts and a BA in International Development and Social Change from Clark University. She has taught poetry and writing in a variety of capacities, including as a teaching artist in schools and nonprofits and as an adjunct instructor at Norwich University. She has also designed and led job skills training programs, directed school plays, and worked as an administrator for an MFA program. She is currently working toward a teaching credential for high school English. Lizzy lives in Vermont with her fiancé and their cat, Rhu. *Red List Blue* is her first book.

www.ingramcontent.com/pod-product-compliance
Lightning Source LLC
Chambersburg PA
CBHW021203090426
42740CB00008B/1208